I Don't Like Reading

by
Lisabeth Emlyn Clark

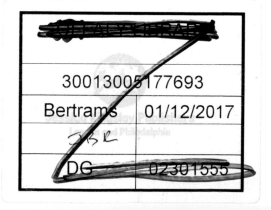

My name is Harry.

I like playing football

and drawing dinosaurs.

I really like playing with my friend Tom.

We swap stickers

and climb trees.

This is **my** little sister Lily.
She can't read yet but

loves looking at books.

Lily always asks **m**e t**o** r**e**ad *her* st**o**ries **b**ut I n**e**ver w**a**nt to,

because i don't
like
reading.

Sometimes the words make me feel all dizzy.

Sometimes the words look so little I can

words look so little I can

hardly

peas all over

see them.

the   world

join hands...

Sometimes

words

really big

all

the

looK

and go

go

BLURRED.

Sometimes I think about having to read the next day, and I can't sleep.

Then I wake up with a tummy ache.

Sometimes I worry about reading aloud in shared reading...

in case I get
muddled and
everyone
laughs.

If there is a lot to read on a page I **?** forget most of it **?** and then have to ● read it all again. If there ... lot to rea... page I forget ... most of it and ... read it

I like writing stories but I get muddled with the words and get cross so I give up.

One night before bed I told
my mum how I felt and she said
not to worry.

She said she would go and
speak to my teacher, Miss
Maurice.

The next day, after school, Mum

and Miss Maurice talked about the

things we could do in class to help me.

Miss Maurice said she would sit with

me and help me

read through

my work.

Miss Maurice spoke to Mr Johnson.
He is the Special Needs
Coordinator.

He showed me different

ways to help me with my reading,

like using

a ruler to put under the words

so I don't

lose my place.

Also I could have someone

reading along with me

until I give them a signal to

stop and I keep going.

Mr Johnson asked a nice lady called Mrs Grace to come and meet me. She is an Educational Psychologist.

She had different games for us to play. We played a game where I had to remember things I'd seen

and the order I'd seen them.

We also played a game where I looked at a picture and had to tell Mrs Grace what was wrong with it.

I really enjoyed this game.

Mrs Grace gave me pages to read on different coloured paper.

We found that, for me, when the words were on green paper, I could read them more clearly.

She **gave** *me* some green see-through plastic called acetate to take with me and use whenever I needed to read something.

A few weeks later my mum
got a letter from Miss Maurice.

It read,

"Harry is a very clever young

boy with a dyslexic profile."

I said, "What's that?"

Mum said it means my brain finds it tricky to understand words and hears them differently, and gets the letters confused and jumbled up.

Mum said that's why I find it harder to spell words and read the books that Tom can.

Mum said it doesn't mean I can't read the books Tom does, it just means I have to try harder.

Me and Mum loOked up dysleXia on her tablet.

We foUnd lots of cleVer, suCcessful peOple with a dyslexiC profile.

I **st**art**e**d writing a liSt

of t**h**em...

Richard Branson

Steve Jobs

Whoopi Goldberg

Kara Tointon

Lewis Hamilton

Rachel Yankey

Jamie Oliver

Now when **Lily** asks me to re**ad** to her th**e** only prob**L**em is...

I don't want to stop.